Which Pet Is Best?

Cameron Macintosh

Which Pet Is Best?

Text: Cameron Macintosh
Publishers: Tania Mazzeo and Eliza Webb
Series consultant: Amanda Sutera
  Hands on Heads Consulting
Editor: Jarrah Moore
Project editor: Annabel Smith
Designer: Leigh Ashforth
Project designer: Danielle Maccarone
Permissions researcher: Liz McShane
Production controller: Renee Tome

Acknowledgements
We would like to thank the following for permission to reproduce copyright material:

Front cover, pp. 2, 4, 6, 7, 8, 23, back cover (dog): iStock.com/JasonDoiy; p. 1, back cover (cat): Shutterstock.com/Eric Isselee; p. 5 (cat): Shutterstock.com/5 second Studio; p. 5, back cover (rabbit): Shutterstock.com/JIANG HONGYAN; p. 5, back cover (guinea pig): Shutterstock.com/Pixel-Shot; p. 5, back cover (axolotl): Alamy Stock Photo/imageBROKER.com GmbH & Co. KG, (chicken): iStock.com/Antagain; pp. 9, 11: iStock.com/vandervelden; p. 10: iStock.com/sdominick; p. 12: iStock.com/fstop123; p. 13: iStock.com/Marcus Lindstrom; p. 14: Shutterstock.com/cynoclub; pp. 15, 16, 17 (bottom): Shutterstock.com/Pixel-Shot; p. 17 (top): Dreamstime.com/Nataliia Kozynska; pp. 18, 20 (main): iStock.com/SilviaJansen; p. 19: iStock.com/VeroniquePeyle; p. 20 (inset): iStock.com/8593; p. 21 (top): iStock.com/Edwin Tan, (main): Shutterstock.com/axolotlowner; p. 22 (top): Dreamstime.com/Sandy Matzen, (bottom): Alamy Stock Photo/imageBROKER.com GmbH & Co. KG; p. 24: Shutterstock.com/JIANG HONGYAN.

NovaStar

Text © 2024 Cengage Learning Australia Pty Limited

ISBN 978 0 17 033394 8

Cengage Learning Australia
Level 5, 80 Dorcas Street
Southbank VIC 3006 Australia
Phone: 1300 790 853
Email: aust.nelsonprimary@cengage.com

For learning solutions, visit **cengage.com.au**

Printed in China by 1010 Printing International Ltd
1 2 3 4 5 6 7 28 27 26 25 24

Nelson acknowledges the Traditional Owners and Custodians of the lands of all First Nations Peoples. We pay respect to Elders past and present, and extend that respect to all First Nations Peoples today.

Contents

Pets

by Jai

Pets can be a lot of fun to have in our lives. They are often great **companions**, and we can learn a lot from looking after them. They can teach us important things like kindness and taking responsibility.

I think a dog is the best pet. However, my friends have other ideas about which animal makes the best pet!

Dogs

Dogs are definitely the best pets!
They are so much fun to be around, and so **loyal**.
My dog, Honey, loves playing in the backyard with me.
She's a good **watchdog**, too. She barks loudly when
someone she doesn't know comes to the house.

Many dogs are very clever.
I've taught Honey lots of tricks and games.
She can shake my hand, give me a high five,
and jump into the air to catch a ball!

Best of all, dogs can be very **affectionate**.
Honey loves to snuggle into my lap
when she is ready for a sleep.

Honey is the best!

Cats

by Zara

I think cats are the best pets by far!
This is my cat, Abby. She likes spending time with me,
but she is also very **independent**. She doesn't seem to mind
being on her own sometimes, so we don't feel bad when we
go out and leave her alone.

Cats are very good at keeping themselves clean.
Abby spends a lot of time cleaning herself.
Unlike a dog, she goes to the toilet in the same place
each time, too – her litter box!

Cats can be such good companions. Abby purrs loudly when I brush her soft fur. She often snuggles up against me when I sit down to read.

Abby is the best pet ever!

Rabbits

by Lucas

Rabbits are the best pets in the world!
My rabbit, Max, is so friendly and cuddly.
He hops straight up to me when I come home from school.

Rabbits are clean and tidy, and they are easy to look after.
Max spends most of the day in a **hutch** in my room,
and he seems very happy there. The hutch door
is always open for him to go in and out.

Rabbits are not only cute, they're clever, too.
I've taught Max a few tricks. He can run through
a little tunnel, and he can even play a game of fetch
with his little ball!

I believe there is no better pet than Max!

Guinea Pigs

by Mina

I think guinea pigs are by far the world's best pets!
My guinea pig, Sam, is very quiet and gentle.
He lets me pick him up and put him on my tummy
while I watch my favourite TV show.

Guinea pigs can be very friendly.
Sam loves it when I give him
pats and scratches.
He even purrs like a cat when
I stroke his fur.

Guinea pigs are quite easy to care for, too.
I just need to keep Sam's hutch clean,
and give him fresh water, hay
and other food to eat each day.
We can feed Sam a lot of
the same vegetables we eat, too.

I would recommend a guinea pig
to anyone!

Chickens

by Archie

I believe chickens are the best pets!
We have lots of chickens, but my favourite is Tabby.
She loves to sit on my lap, and she really enjoys pats, too.

Chickens are easy to care for. I don't need to take my chickens for a walk or brush them. We just need to make sure their food and water containers are always full.

It's very useful to have chickens in the backyard.
Our chickens eat lots of our food scraps, which
saves us from throwing the scraps in the bin.
Our chickens lay eggs that we can eat, too.

Chickens are definitely the best pets!

Axolotls

by Grace

I think my axolotl (say: *ax-a-lot-ul*), Tiny,
is the best pet ever! Axolotls are also known as
walking fish, because they can walk under
the water as well as swim. Tiny isn't the kind
of pet that I can pat, because she needs to stay
in her tank, but she is a **unique** animal.

Tiny is beautiful to look at. I love the feathery shape of her **gills**. I also love the shape of her mouth, which makes her look like she's smiling all the time.

Another thing I love about Tiny is that she is easy to look after. I enjoy feeding her and watching her eat. Her favourite foods are tiny **shrimps** and worms.

Axolotls are the best pets ever!

Perfect Pets

My friends and I don't quite agree on which animal makes the best pet! However, we do agree that all pets are special, and they deserve the very best care we can give them.

There is a perfect pet for everyone.

Glossary

affectionate (*adjective*)	friendly or loving
companions (*noun*)	animals or people you spend a lot of time with
gills (*noun*)	small flaps on the sides of a fish or an amphibian's body
hutch (*noun*)	a special house for small animals
independent (*adjective*)	happy to be alone
loyal (*adjective*)	staying with someone in good and bad times
shrimps (*noun*)	small sea animals
unique (*adjective*)	not like anything else
watchdog (*noun*)	a dog that watches for danger to a house

Index